BEST.LIFE.EVER.
THE BOOK

~~fine~~
~~okay-ish~~
~~good enough~~

BEST.LIFE.EVER.
THE BOOK

12 Steps to Stop **REACTING** to Life
& Begin **CREATING** It

The self-guided version of the life-changing course by
JOANNA RAJENDRAN

Copyright © 2025 by Joanna Rajendran
www.joannarajendran.com

All rights reserved. This book or any portion thereof may not be reproduced or used in any manner whatsoever without the express written permission of the publisher except for the use of brief quotations in articles and book reviews.

NO AI TRAINING: Without in any way limiting the author's [and publisher's] exclusive rights under copyright, any use of this publication to "train" generative artificial intelligence (AI) technologies to generate text is expressly prohibited. The author reserves all rights to license uses of this work for generative AI training and development of machine learning language models.

First Printing, 2025

ISBN-13: 978-1-962984-90-4 print edition
ISBN-13: 978-1-962984-91-1 ebook edition

Waterside Productions
2055 Oxford Ave
Cardiff, CA 92007
www.waterside.com

To every beautiful soul who has taken the BEST.LIFE.EVER. course. Thank you for trusting me with your dreams. And to YOU, brave reader, for being bold enough to embrace yours.

To my big crazy family, I am me because you are you and we are all the luckiest.

And to my dreams in human form: my forever date my Dude, our world-changer Natasha Tao, and our sweet-souled River Vail; everything, always, for you.

Contents

Preface: Don't Quit Your Daydream ix
Introduction: Who, What, Why & How xi

Chapter 1: Be Present 1
Chapter 2: Exorcise Limiting Beliefs 7
Chapter 3: (4) Steps to Manifesting 13
Chapter 4: Thirty-Day Letter 19
Chapter 5: Let's Start the Day 29
Chapter 6: Inflating Your Bubble of Awesome 37
Chapter 7: Focus on Your Words 43
Chapter 8: Expanding Your Practice 49
Chapter 9: Empowering Partnerships 57
Chapter 10: Virtue of Giving It Away (Pay It Forward) 63
Chapter 11: Emerging As I Am 69
Chapter 12: Relive & Recap 75

Epilogue: Dream On 85
Acknowledgments 87

Preface

Don't Quit Your Daydream

You! Yes, YOU! You with the book in your hand. You, who saw a title called **BEST.LIFE.EVER.** and realized there is no one more deserving than you to experience just that. You, who, whether your life has been fairly enjoyable or whether you have been in a current season of challenge, recognize that there is a version of your life that could be even more satisfying.

You are an amazing, gorgeous, sparkly souled human that is worth everything. (If you need further convincing, just try googling the odds of the specific meeting of a particular sperm with a certain egg to create the miracle that is you! SPOILER ALERT—it's approximately 1 in 250 million!)

At some point, typically during our childhood, we envision our lives in full Technicolor brilliance. We see our ideal version of our present and our future filled with personal, professional, physical, and relationship magic. We can see the love we are capable of giving and the love we so deserve to receive.

And then what happens?

Yup—you guessed it. That four-letter word called L-I-F-E. We are conditioned through typical education and cultural and societal expectations to sit in chairs, to passively receive instruction, to be "practical" and "realistic." We are taught information to pass the corresponding test. We are told to be good, which far too often translates to "be like everyone else." We are encouraged to choose a focus of study at a young age and then surprised if it doesn't match who or what we evolve into. We are training generations of people to confuse their identity with their profession, their value with their wealth, and their importance with their influence.

And socially, we are increasing the slope of that uphill battle. We are living in an age where we are constantly connected and lonely; always reachable and overwhelmed; overinformed and unimpressed; and hyperstimulated and uninspired. We are learning to grade and judge our achievements and compete with one another. Through social media, the temptation to compare yourself to everyone else is reinforced. And as the old adage states that "comparison is the thief of joy," the feeling of "not-enough" is reaching epic proportions.

And the worst part—all this busyness that we have learned to wear as a badge of honor is negatively impacting our health, our relationships, and our feelings of happiness.

With technology making it so that we are always "on," we have lost one of the biggest gifts: boredom. It is when we are bored, in the moments between, that our imaginations have the opportunity to go wild. That is where some of our greatest ideas, our best "downloads," come from.

SO BACK TO YOU, BRAVE SOUL! Given all of that, something has inspired enough curiosity for you to choose this book and to have gotten through this opening so ... CONGRATULATIONS!

The notion that you intuitively know that there is another option indicates that you are already rocking life. You are reconnecting with that part of you that already knows. The part that knows who you are, how you are, and the incredible life that is waiting for you when you express your unique gifts in this world.

There is something that only you, with your perspective, in your voice, through the lens of your experiences, can offer. I am thrilled, through this book, to spend a bit of time together, reminding you of that gift and then offering some actionable tools and suggested habits around it to help you reconnect with that version of your life that you used to, or may still do, see as your greatest. The version that sets your soul on fire.

The version that is YOUR specific, unique **BEST.LIFE.EVER.**

Thank you for trusting me with your magic. It is a supreme honor to remind you of your PEACE, POWER & POSSIBILITY ...

—Joanna

Introduction

Who, What, Why & How

Perhaps we should begin at the beginning . . .

WHO

BEST.LIFE.EVER. was a course originally developed by me, Joanna Rajendran. My titles have included: Mindset Mastery Coach, Meditation Expert, Yoga Teacher, Keynote Speaker, and author of the must-read book (if I do say so myself) *My Guru Wears Heels.* After spending twenty-six years studying with and learning from a modern-day sage, I shared the incredible story of my time with Master Teacher Tao Porchon-Lynch and the lessons learned in what I hoped to be a raw and relatable way. After the launch of my book, I was inspired to take these teachings out of the studios and bring them into the world. The only issue—just a tiny global pandemic. Along with my Dude and our two kids, we decided to run away and move to the beach. From this newfound paradise, **BEST.LIFE.EVER.**—the virtual twelve-week course that offered habits of success and happiness—was born.

WHAT

The happy accident of having the course be virtual was that unlike when you go on a retreat and feel fully present to your peace and power only to experience what I refer to as the "retreat hangover" when attempting to re-enter "normal" life, meeting weekly and spending the intervening seven days practicing the action steps allowed for the magic to happen within the context of your real life! The resulting transformations were incredible to witness!

WHY

Perhaps you are thinking this all sounds great, but what's in it for you? Valid question. Our time is our most precious commodity. If you are going to spend even a bit of it reading this book, it would help to know what you could expect to receive in return. Well, the answer is simple. If there is any part of you that wants to BE, GIVE, HAVE or DO **MORE** in your life than you currently are, you have come to the right place. You know those moments when everything is in alignment; when all the lights turn green, when you think of someone and they call, when you see a rainbow, your favorite song comes on the radio, and so on? THAT is what it feels like when you are living fully expressed.

But don't take my word for it. See if you could see a bit of yourself in any of the following real-life clients' experiences.

- *"Best. Life. Ever. literally changed my life. It's pure magic. The strategies have changed me forever and I'm so grateful for these teachings." —Jackie (repeat client, actress, and mom/advocate)*

- *"I seriously feel so free right now. I am definitely a walking testimonial. Lost sight of my mental health and made a huge leap in just six weeks." —Beth (banker, mom, and small business owner)*

- *"Thank you for the reminder that anything is possible, and that people are simply amazing! This course made me feel like me again. And I'm so grateful. Because honestly, I like me. And I was dimmed for a bit." —Carrie (health and wellness professional, single mom extraordinaire)*

- *"Every person, from every walk of life, at every age... deserves this course." —Adam (media consultant, business owner)*

HOW

The signature course **BEST.LIFE.EVER.** was designed to be twelve weekly, one-hour virtual sessions. Each group is like a unicorn, uniquely different as the energy of the course is shaped by the collective vibe of the souls who join. It often begins as a disparate group of individuals who, by the end, have formed a true and beautiful community. In this book, though we cannot recreate the immersive group dynamic experienced through the live weekly interactions, I've committed to providing you with the integral concepts, actionable tools, and mindset mastery techniques that can and will enhance your sense of joy, happiness, and satisfaction.

Are you ready? If so, my suggestion to you is to play full out. Whether you read each chapter and pause to play with the action step or barrel full steam ahead, your pace is your choice. You may choose to go about this journey on your own, invite a partner or loved one to join, or even form a small group to experience it together. In any case, the intention is that you enjoy the process, benefit from the exercises, and that you connect with what sets your SOUL ON FIRE! Because when that happens and you feel that level of joy, every relationship in your life and every interaction in your day will benefit. The ripple of your peace, your love, your you-ness, will be larger than you can even imagine. And hey, if we truly aspire for world peace, what is that? A world filled with peaceful individuals. So let's start with you.

Are you ready?

LET'S GO!

Chapter 1
BEST.LIFE.EVER

Be Present

"Live the actual moment. Only this actual moment is life."
—Thich Nhat Hanh

BEHAVIOR

When was the last time you uni-tasked? If pressed, many of us might find it challenging to recall the last time we gave our complete, undistracted attention to a single task. Too often, we are listening to a podcast while working out; helping kids with homework while cooking; texting while driving; answering emails while in another meeting. Single-minded focus has become the exception rather than the rule. So the notion of carving out time to do less—to sit and dream, to connect with your breath, to meditate—may seem like a daunting task.

You may have even come up with reasons that it doesn't work for you. In my time coaching, I've heard everything from "I just can't clear my head" to "I don't have the time" to "I can't sit still" or the classic "I'm just not good at meditating." If any of those sound familiar, be assured, you are in good company. The good news is that it is far simpler than you may think. In yoga, there is a concept called "beginner's mind." If you think about what it's like to do something brand new, it is a very present experience. Because we have no existing frame of reference, we tend to bring our full attention to new tasks. We bring a sense of wonder, a childlike naïveté to what is brand new. In fact, yoga is called a practice because it was never intended to be something that we could finish or complete. The magic is truly in the journey rather than the destination. Similarly, when attempting to find your peace, your stillness, it's helpful to engage that same concept of beginner's mind.

While this chapter is not about meditating per se, it is about finding space between our thoughts to truly connect with the present moment and how and who we are being within that context. We are going to begin our journey together by assessing where we really are in this present moment and specifically, where it is in relation to where we want to be.

We are whole beings, and as a result, the approach we take to creating our **BEST.LIFE.EVER.** must be a holistic one. Each chapter will offer its own **B.L.E.**—a **behavior**, a **lesson**, and an **exercise**. In some chapters, you may be inspired to look at the exercises through the lens of your profession while others might inspire you to see it from another perspective: personal, physical, romantic, interpersonal, and so on. The fact is that even if you are specifically drawn to creating your life by design as it pertains to one area of your life, it is impossible to do so without impacting the others.

📝 LESSON
TOWARD & AWAY

How do you know what constitutes your **BEST.LIFE.EVER.** and if you are getting closer to living it? One question that could get you close, if not all the way, to your answer is a version of the following: If money and time were no object, what would you spend your life doing? Who would you be doing it with? Where would you be living? Would you work? Pursue your passions? Your philanthropy? Take that improv class? Buy a boat? Profess your love to someone?

_____
_____
_____
_____
_____
_____
_____
_____
_____
_____
_____
_____
_____
_____
_____
_____
_____

Whether you had an immediate and definitive answer to that question or whether it's more of a general feeling you are searching for, there are some clues to consider.

We all have within us an inner guidance system. Call it intuition, a gut feeling, an inner knowing; whatever it is, it contains so many of the answers to many of our questions. To illustrate, if you've ever walked down a street only to get a warning from that inner guide in the form of hair standing up on the back of your neck, a pit in your stomach, your heart beating faster with worry, you've already experienced it.

Conversely, the opposite is also true. We get physiological cues when things are in alignment; feeling calmed by a hug, happy butterflies of excitement, the tingle of seeing someone you love.

Put simply, these feelings can be summed up in terms of AHHH (like your body heaving a sigh) or UGGHH (tension experienced as physical anxiety). To help identify how and where these principles work in your life, play with the following exercise.

EXERCISE

Breathe in a full, deep breath until your lungs expand like a balloon. Pause in that moment of fullness. Sip in a bit more breath. Now, exhale slowly. Let the breath seep out of you, taking with it any tension you've collected. Notice how you feel. If it's anything less than peaceful, do that again until you feel that full-body sigh.

Notice when tension arises, where it lives in your physical form. Conversely, when you feel truly peaceful, where do those warm fuzzies exist? Knowing your physiological cues will help you to enhance more of what you love and identify less of what you don't.

- Spend the next twenty-four hours jotting down the people, events, and circumstances that give you the feeling of ***ahhhh***.

_____
_____
_____
_____
_____
_____

- Spend the next twenty-four hours jotting down the people, events, and circumstances that give you the feeling of ***ughhhh***.

_____
_____
_____
_____
_____
_____
_____

The people, events, and circumstances in your world are either leading you **toward** or **away** from the best version of your life. It is important to identify them in our desire to curate experiences, relationships, and opportunities to begin to stack the odds in the **toward** column.

CHAPTER 2
BEST.LIFE.EVER.

Exorcise Limiting Beliefs

"The only limits you have are the limits you believe."
—Wayne Dyer

BEHAVIOR

Have you ever gone to do something... and been either hindered or guided by your own thoughts? We all have a voice that lives inside our heads. Sometimes that voice can be our best cheerleader, reminding us that we can achieve what we set out to do. Far too often, however, that voice can be our inner critic, causing us to doubt our ideas, or even worse, our ability to execute them. This is the voice behind those feelings of *not enough*.

If prompted, could you recall the last compliment you were paid? If so, did you believe what was said about you? In contrast, if you were asked about an insult someone made to or about you when you were just a kid, could that answer come quickly? We have a tendency to recall, and even worse, believe, the negative things we hear about ourselves more than the positive.

WHY?

What is the origin story of that doubt? When we hear our mental naysayer, is it even our voice that's speaking? Or is it that of an old boss, a family member, a teacher, a friend?

Our shared intention through this book is to create our lives with purpose and with power. The first step is recognizing what indicates we're moving toward it or what brings us farther away—as you did in the first chapter. Chapter 2 is all about excavating and releasing that which no longer serves us so that we can build the new on a solid foundation. Consider it like cleaning out the room before filling it with new furniture.

📝 LESSON

Getting to the heart of the inner critic is hardly comfortable, but the rewards are worth the effort. Answer the following questions as honestly and authentically as possible for maximum benefits.

- What is a story you've been telling about yourself that no longer serves you?

_____
_____
_____
_____
_____
_____
_____

- What is the origin of that story? Was it based on something that actually happened or on your interpretation of events?

_____
_____
_____
_____
_____
_____
_____

- Who was the original voice in your story?

___

- How would you feel if you released the hold this story has had on you?

___

🏋 Exercise

By answering the questions above, you may have illuminated an incident that has played a significant role in the choices you've made in your life. Too often, we conflate our notion of who we are with the things that happen to us. Distinguishing between the two helps us reclaim our identity by choice—who we really are in our core.

Many of us have had something like this occur in our lives, and it becomes our "Voldemort." For those who are not Harry Potter fans, he is the villain who they begin to call "He-Who-Must-Not-Be-Named." His darkness was so feared that the thought was that by simply saying his name out loud, you'd help bring about the darkness. Then, along came the young Harry who thought that by not saying his name, by fearing to name the thing, he was actually giving him more power. If you think of your Voldemort—the thing that seems too painful to relive, to talk about, to think about—chances are that it hasn't released its grip on you. It likely just comes up in the quieter moments; the longer car rides or the middle-of-the-night thoughts. In this exercise, we are going to consciously choose the opposite approach. Instead of sweeping this transformative event or memory under the proverbial rug any longer, we are going to bring it into the light to lessen its hold.

WRITE IT

What was a negative or difficult event that shaped the trajectory of your life and has become something you don't like to think or talk about but is still impacting your idea of who you are?

- Have you already thought of it?
- Once you have, use this space (or another piece of paper if you don't like to rip pages from books) and describe the event.
- Use as much detail as you can so that reading it engages as many of your senses as possible.

_____
_____
_____
_____
_____
_____
_____
_____
_____
_____
_____
_____
_____
_____
_____

RELEASE IT

Now that you've intentionally thought about something you usually suppress and have written about it in what was likely more detail than you would consciously choose to remember, what do you do with this letter?

- **STEP 1:** Read it. Out loud. If there is someone with whom you feel safe and comfortable, you may ask them to simply hold space for you as your listener.* If you choose this path, be sure to ask them to just listen, offering no verbal or physical signs of comfort. After you read it to them, if there is any negative feeling, read it again. Continue this process until you finish a round of reading and experience neutral emotions. (You will know when you've achieved this feeling of neutrality by how you FEEL when you finish reading the letter.)

    If you do NOT wish to use a partner for this, the same exercise can be done by reading your letter out loud in front of a mirror.

- **STEP 2:** Physically destroy the letter. Some people prefer to rip their letter to shreds while others like to burn it. The important thing is that you symbolically reclaim the power this story has held over you by first saying your Voldemort aloud until the sting doesn't sting as much and then by physically eliminating its existence.

After decades of teaching and taking workshops in the personal development arena, this trauma letter exercise has been one of the most exceptional. It is so simple in concept that you may be tempted to question the profound nature of its impact. To that I would simply respond that it is worth a shot. If it doesn't work, you are exactly where you already were. But when it does . . . you will experience the peace of mind that comes from muting the inner critic and stopping the old movie from playing on repeat in your mind.

CHAPTER 3
BE**S**T.LIFE.EVER.

(4) Steps to Manifesting

"Ask for what you want and be prepared to get it."
—Maya Angelou

BEHAVIOR

When we are young, we unapologetically go after what we want. If you think back to your childhood, you could likely recall a time when you wanted something so badly that you just knew that it would happen. Maybe it was a physical object, like the bicycle with the banana seat and the ribbons that streamed from the handlebars or the video game your neighborhood friend had. Perhaps it was an experience: going to an amusement park, seeing a new movie, having a sleepover at your friend's house. Regardless of what it was that was desired, without ever being taught how, we intuitively knew how to harness the power of manifesting*—of turning thought into thing, desire into result.

*If the word manifest is too woo woo for you, feel free to swap the word out with something more innocuous like create.

So what happened? Somehow along the way, we've learned to complicate this process. We have bought into the flawed premise that the outcome could only be the result of an arduous journey. This message is reinforced by notions that we must sacrifice for what we desire.

What if you discovered that the opposite was true? That it was not only possible, but even more effective, to manifest with ease? That the time it takes for something to go from your imagination into your reality does not have to be long, hard, or riddled with sacrifice and compromise?

To help make it possible for you to get right into playing with this concept in your life, we will break it down into four simple steps.

📝 LESSON

STEP 1

- ### *ASK*

Logically, we know that to get what we want, we first must know what that is. What is it that you truly desire? And as you answer, note that specificity with language and clarity of vision is vital. There is nothing too big nor too small to be an ask.

> EXAMPLE: You are launching a new app, and you want it to be a huge success. You might say something like, "Please let this app launch, and I want to make a lot of money." Sounds simple enough, right? What if the outcome was that the app launched, had some glitches, and didn't work? But you also lost a relative who left you a bunch of money. Was that your desired outcome? Technically, it checks all the boxes of what you were seeking and yet, were that the result, you might be tempted to think that this process of manifesting didn't work. This is an example of how important it is to be clear in both the actual vision and in the language you attach to it. In the example above, how could you ask in a clearer, more effective way? Something like, "Please let this app be a huge and satisfying success; a source of personal and professional pride, wealth, and joy."

STEP 2

• BELIEVE

Your outcome will never exceed your belief. Even if we pose the best question for the result we desire, we must actually believe it is possible. And not just possible, but possible for US! Let's continue with the example of the launch of an app. If you've created one and are about to go to market, do you see it, feel it, and believe it to be a success? Have you envisioned how satisfied you feel as you celebrate the launch? Can you see it solving the specific problem and serving the intended community you sought?

If you find that this is the step that poses a challenge—that you lack belief—it almost always comes down to a question of worth. You have to know that if you have the idea in your mind or in your heart that inspired the ensuing action you took, you are worthy! And if you still don't believe that, perhaps the following two questions will help strengthen your sense of worthiness to receive it...

- Does what you want already exist in this world? Because if the answer is yes, then it's possible. More importantly, if it's possible for anyone, why not you?
- If evidence of what you are asking doesn't yet exist, it stands to reason that someone has to be the first. Why can't it be you?

STEP 3

• RELEASE

To recap, you are on Step 3 because you have already asked (with clarity and specificity) and you believe that your ask will happen and that you are worthy of the result. So what is Step 3 and why does it pose a challenge for some? This is the point in the process where we *let go*. Why is that so hard? Because this was meaningful enough to us that we asked in the first place and important enough that we worked to shore up our belief that it will happen.

You know the WHAT. Step 3 is about releasing attachment to the HOW. And more so, it's important to leave room for the magic. In fact, imagine that you are getting in your car to drive somewhere, and you enter the address into your GPS. If the system suggests that you change routes to save twenty minutes, you're likely to agree. It wasn't the path that you were committing to, it was the destination. When we are manifesting our dreams, we want to leave space for the myriad ways the universe will conspire to help us make them a reality. Let's consider the example of the app launch. You may have had the innovative concept for the app. Does that mean you have to personally have the IT knowledge to develop it and the marketing expertise to launch it? No. We can partner with people with complementary skills. More than that though, when we try and control the how, we may overlook the things that appear as coincidence or divine intervention along the way that take our dreams from thought to thing. Perhaps a casual chat with a friend leads to a connection with a tech publication that results in an interview that gives your app the exposure it needs to gain traction. Six months later, you have a wildly successful product and opportunity to expand or sell.

Because the unfolding is important to us, we are often tempted to hyper-control the way it goes. This is a fallacy because even the most creative minds cannot imagine the way it will actually unfold. Our time is better spent elsewhere.

Where? you may wonder. We are better served to spend time doing something that puts us in the feeling of the outcome than trying to control how it comes.

What does that mean in practical terms? If you want to feel like the successful CEO of the app you launched, do things that already inspire feelings of success and satisfaction. If you want to connect with the feeling of wealth, go to an area of life where you already feel "wealthy"—whether that's in the sector of love, in your friendships, or maybe looking at a vibrant investment account. If you want to feel present to your success, revel in an area of your life where you already feel wildly successful. The same can be applied whether your ask was regarding finding romantic love, having great health, traveling more, and so on. While your request is loading, you are best served doing activities or being in environments that already trigger the feelings you'd experience had your dream already come true: daydreaming about waking up in love, doing a workout that makes you feel strong, going on a hike, and so on.

STEP 4

• THANK

This step may seem so obvious that it can be overlooked. But the importance of gratitude in our lives and in the steps to manifesting cannot be overstated! It is the vital component to completing one cycle before pressing rinse and repeat for the next ask. We want to pause and revel in the notion that what was once a dream has actually come to fruition. We want to use this moment of celebration to encourage continuation.

Being truly grateful for what has happened is our way of putting the cherry on top of the ice cream. It also gives us the chance to take stock of the miracles in our lives. We begin to compile the "good stuff," and that shifts what we grow to expect: more of the good in our lives. This step is so simple to do but also so simple that you may be tempted to overlook it.

EXERCISE

(1) **ASK** What are you asking for?

_____
_____
_____
_____

(2) **BELIEVE** Do you believe it is possible? Have you seen examples of it happening before? Do you know that you are worthy of receiving it?

_____
_____
_____
_____

(3) RELEASE What is an area that already feels good? That feels like how you'd feel if you were already in the result of your request? Go to that area and play. (Give an example.)

_____
_____
_____
_____
_____

(4) THANK Express, in detail, your feelings of gratitude that it happened, how it happened, and how you feel about it happening.

_____
_____
_____
_____
_____

CHAPTER 4
BEST.LIFE.EVER.

Thirty-Day Letter

"I planned my success. I knew it was going to happen."
—Erykah Badu

BEHAVIOR

Let's consider an incredibly satisfying time in your life. What made it so? Did the magic simply unfold? Was it the result of time and effort? Or did everything seem to just fall into place at once? Did you even realize how great everything was then, or was it only upon reflection after the season had passed?

What if there was a way to not only anticipate the next round of blessings, but also to place your specific requests almost as if you were asking a DJ to play your favorite songs? What if it began to feel that instead of responding to the events, people, and circumstances that life threw your way, you were actively and consciously choosing them?

In this chapter, we will discuss one the most effective tools in the **BEST.LIFE.EVER.** tool belt—the thirty-day letter. We will share how this simple practice of intentionally scripting your story and then creating a ritual around it can effectively shift your hope into vision and your wish into an expectation. Does the notion of that excite you? Perhaps it would be helpful to share some of the success stories from **BEST.LIFE.EVER.** participants who have used this tool to enhance their lives...

- Nicole used her thirty-day letter to detail what life would look like once she found her dream career. Instead of focusing on what she perceived would be her obstacles (not having a degree in that specific field and taking years off to be a stay-at-home mom), she wrote, in detail, about how proud she felt to be in her new role. She wrote about what it looked like balancing mom life and career so well, how great she felt dressing for work, and how confident she felt with her new coworkers. Not only did her entire letter come true, but it also came with an even more exciting title and bigger paycheck than she had hoped.

- Beth dreamed of a specific house she wanted to buy in a small neighborhood in a suburb of NY in the midst of a tight real estate market. And the kicker—the house wasn't even on the market. She used her letter to paint the picture of what it would be like to pull into the driveway of their forever home, to see her kids playing basketball out front, to take their dog for walks in the neighborhood, for her husband to have a dedicated office. She wrote in detail, embracing the feeling of pride she felt living in their dream home and having it be the backdrop for their memories. By the time the thirty days ended, they were under contract and now live in the exact house.

- For years, Ilene had felt the love of her children, her grandchildren, her colleagues, and her wide circle of friends. She was even best friends with her ex-husband, whom she'd divorced decades earlier. The only love she didn't have was romantic love. When pressed by her daughters, her response was always the same, saying that ship had sailed. When writing her thirty-day letter, Ilene decided that she was going to write about the notion of welcoming love into her life. She wrote about a partner who enjoyed the same things she did, who was kind, and with whom she'd like to spend her time. About a week later, a friend asked if they could introduce to her someone, and the two have been together ever since.

✏️ LESSON

Why has the thirty-day letter become such a fan favorite of almost everyone who has taken the course? The answer is because it is so simple to do and yet the impact is absolutely limitless. Now let's get into how it works.

HOW

In the thirty-day letter, we write a letter from the perspective of thirty days into the future. The letter can be in the format of a journal entry, directed to yourself, or written to a higher power. (Personally, I tend to write it as I would if it were a diary entry—real, honest, and with the expectation that it is for my eyes only.) The intention of the letter is to highlight and celebrate all that has transpired in the previous month. The letter details not only what has happened, but it also highlights the feelings of satisfaction you experience as a result.

WHY

When we write our life in this way—from the vantage point of the near future looking back on what has recently occurred—we focus on all that we wanted to happen. Doing it in this format shifts what we seek from being something we aspire to happen to being what we are celebrating because it already has happened. Keep in mind that our brains do not distinguish between real and imagined. We are harnessing that to program our minds to not only WISH for a desired result but also to actually EXPECT it. And we do it in digestible, thirty-day chunks of time. Before we begin putting pen to paper, let's go over some suggested things to do and not to do as you write your letter.

DOs ✅

- ***Think big!***

If there is no distinction between the energy it requires to create a building or a button, why not go for the building? Often, we think in the reverse, seeking proof of concept before going all in. We may think it's safer to start small, with something we don't care about as much, before going for the important items. I challenge you to use this letter to detail the best possible version rather than the safe, less lofty version.

- ## Watch your words!

When you write, be sure to use the language of everything you truly desire rather than the absence of what you don't want. While that might seem obvious, this is one that is easy to miss if not intentional. For example, if you are undergoing treatment for cancer and you write that you are *cancer free*, you are still putting the word cancer into your letter. Cancer is not what you are seeking. *Healthy, vibrant cells, unlimited energy, and gorgeous scans* may be examples of what you could write in its place. The same goes for those looking to increase their finances. Instead of writing *get out of debt*, you want to phrase it in the presence of what you do want—more money than you could spend, use, donate, share, and so on. Or it could be a feeling such as *I open the bank app on my phone to see that every account has double the amount it had last month. It feels incredibly satisfying to know that I can afford all that I want to do and to have money flowing to me from so many sources.*

- ## Activate the senses using tenses!

While I encourage you to use past tense when detailing the events that transpired in the previous thirty days, I suggest using the present tense when writing about the resulting feelings. For example, *We closed on the house of our dreams. The transaction was seamless, and the process was easy. I feel such an overwhelming feeling of pride as I hold the keys to our first home. Walking through our front door for the first time was a special experience. I am so proud to call this place our home.* Writing of the action is in the past tense as we want to celebrate that it occurred, using this exercise of reverse engineering. The feelings about the action are in the present so that as we read it, it may wash over us again and intensify the satisfaction.

- ## *Include your loved ones*

Can your letter include other people in your life? Absolutely. We do not live our lives in isolation, and therefore our dreams tend to include those we love. That said, while we can detail things happening in the lives around us, the focus is really on how that makes us feel. To illustrate, if you are a parent, your happiness is intrinsically linked to the happiness of your children. So you may write something like *My daughter started her new school. The transition was smoother than we thought; she loved her new teacher and made two new friends. She is so happy. Seeing her settled, happy, and thriving makes me feel calm in our choice. I love hearing her excitedly share her stories of the day at dinner each night.*

DO NOTs ✗

- ## *People please!*

We already touched on the notion that it requires the same energy to create a building or a button, but this point is so worth the extra focus. Even if you think you're writing about your dreams, are they the real ones? Or is it the version you've been taught to want and expect? We can, if unchecked, be unduly influenced by what our family, community, or even society expects from us. It is important to distinguish between the logical, expected dream and our soul's true desire. For instance, perhaps you have a very lucrative and successful career in something that you do quite well. When you learn that you are next in line for a high-level position, it might be expected that that would be the desired result. What if you've been considering a career change and are ready to pursue something that sets your soul on fire? This letter is for YOU, not the version of what you think is expected of you. Be sure to use it as the manifesting tool of YOUR dreams!

- ## *Limit yourself!*

For purposes of this exercise (and perhaps even in general), let's get that dreaded r-word out of our vocabulary. What is the r-word, you ask? *Realistic.* The only limit to what is possible in our lives is that which we create for ourselves about ourselves. If you knew that it was all possible, what would you really include in this letter? THAT! That is the version we encourage you to write in this chapter.

- **_Make yourself the supporting character!_**

While we have already touched on the notion that it is not only acceptable but it is also quite likely that your letter will include those you love, let's be sure to keep yourself as the main character in your own movie. In fact, not only is that not selfish but it is also an important thing to model for those around you. How else can we expect those whom we love, live with, and guide to remember the importance of boldly going after their dreams if we are too busy putting everyone else first to go after our own?

- **_Embrace technology!_**

There are so many helpful uses of our everyday gadgets. As such, you may be tempted to use your phone to write your letter. Don't! This letter is important. Our language is carefully chosen and intentional. It isn't the time to risk autocorrect predicting, or worse, changing our words. Also, there is something special that comes from having our thoughts travel from our mind and heart into our hand and through the pen onto paper. When we read our letters, that magic is enhanced by seeing our words, written in our writing, detailing our dreams. That said, a great use of the phone is to take a photo of your letter once complete. That way, if you are traveling or in bed with a sleeping partner, you can have the letter handy and easy to read.

🏋 EXERCISE

Before you begin writing your first thirty-day letter, we encourage you to do something to prepare—to get in state. This could be a grounding practice such as a walk in the woods or sitting on the grass. It could be something that brings up joy: a phone call with your best friend, a dance party in your kitchen. Or it could simply be closing your eyes and taking a few rounds of deep, cleansing breaths.

From that place, in your state of being present, write your letter.

Chapter 4: Thirty-Day Letter

Joanna Rajendran

Chapter 4: Thirty-Day Letter

ACTIVATING YOUR THIRTY-DAY LETTER

The final step to this practice once you've written your letter is to activate it. We do so by creating a daily ritual around reading it at two specific points in our day.

AWAKE, STRETCH, READ. . .

As soon as you wake up in the morning, begin your day by reading your letter. If we want to shift from responding to creating our days, months, and lives with intention and purpose, it is crucial that we read our letter first thing. This is before checking the phone, the inbox, text messages, the news, and so on. Those all serve to put us in the mode of *reacting* to what the world needs from us—the direct opposite of *creating* what it is that we want in our world. Consider reading your letter first thing in the morning akin to setting the frequency on your radio so that you are tuned in to the station you want to hear. This is a method of priming the mind to focus on the version of our lives that we want the most. By tuning our focus this way, it makes us way more likely to recognize the mini miracles that will happen along the way to the things in our letters coming true.

SWEET DREAMS, BUT FIRST. . .

Thomas Edison used to fall asleep in a chair while holding a ball. As he nodded off, the grip on the ball would loosen, and the ball would fall to the floor waking him up. The moment it did, he jotted down notes in his notebook. This practice was done because he must have recognized how magical that in-between state was: the place between dreaming and being awake. When we read our letters right before going to sleep, we benefit from this creative state of being. We also have the ability to program our subconscious as to what we want to focus on as we sleep. If you think of a time you fell asleep after watching the news or a scary movie and had an unpleasant dream, you will realize how much power we have to influence our thoughts to work for us during the night. By reading our letter right before bed, we can program our subconscious so that the thoughts and images we think and see as we sleep are those that represent our **BEST.LIFE.EVER.**

CHAPTER 5
BEST.LIFE.EVER.

Let's Start the Day

"Morning is an important time of the day, because how you spend your morning can often tell you what kind of day you are going to have."
—Lemony Snicket

BEHAVIOR

BZZZ BZZZ BZZZ.

BZZZ BZZZ BZZZ.

BZZZ BZZZ BZZZ.

It's a brand-new day. And how do you know? Is it because as you stretch your arms and place your feet on the ground, the birds are chirping, the sun is shining, and the sky is a radiant shade of blue?

Theoretically, most of us would concede the point that starting our day with good habits, with joy, and with purpose would be a positive choice. So why is that not the case for so many?

Do you currently begin each day in a way that fuels you, fills you with enthusiasm while grounding you in a centered peace? Or do you know it's morning because the sound of the alarm just invaded your dreams, and you responded by hitting the snooze button until your body is now hijacked by the anxious feeling of rushing and by the worry of running late? Do you robotically grab your phone and see the news scroll, the text alerts, the email messages before you crawl zombie-like to get the slug of coffee that helps you shed enough of the brain fog to proceed with your day on autopilot?

If you are identifying with the latter rather than the former, congratulations! Being honest about where you are is a necessary step in identifying if it's working for you. And, if it's not, it is a crucial step in determining what to do about it.

Almost every successful leader credits a morning ritual as one of the factors in their continued success. They recognize the importance of a consistent routine that would engage the senses, focus their minds, and create the day with purpose and intention.

Imagine what such a routine could do in your life. If you think it sounds great but wouldn't know where to begin, keep reading!

LESSON

If you identified with the example above—waking up to the alarm, perhaps after snoozing, only to scramble to get out of the house both rushing and exhausted—the notion of adding more to your morning may sound daunting. What if you learned that with very little actual time, you could feel so much better? What if you discovered that instead of dragging your body out of bed, you could jump out of it with your soul on fire? That you won't be able to wait one more moment before beginning another day in this beautiful life of yours?

First, let's check in.

YOUR CURRENT PRACTICE

Whether you realize it or not, you currently have a morning ritual. It is one you've either consciously chosen or one that has become a habit by default. Are you waking up an hour early to go for a run or meditate? Are you driving to work on autopilot hardly remembering how you got there? Are you enjoying the morning with your family at breakfast before parting ways? Whatever it is, use this space to honestly describe how you *begin* a typical day.

THE IMPACT

Describe below how this routine is impacting you. Are you exhausted? Do you feel excited for the thrill and newness of the new day? Are you overwhelmed and wondering how you'll get everything done? Are you swimming in gratitude or feeling defeated? Use this space to share how you *feel* as you begin a typical day.

Taking an honest look at where you are compared to where you'd like to be is a crucial step in creating the version of your life that you most want. And remember, your life is a compilation of your days. Left unchecked, your days can choose you. In contrast, by choosing a morning ritual that works for you and practicing it consistently, you can create the energy of your day thereby changing the feeling of your entire life. It is THAT worthwhile to do. Hopefully, the following exercises can assist you in the process.

🏋 EXERCISE

Together we can create a happy morning checklist that can increase the joy you experience daily without requiring big chunks of time. Whether you question if this will work or are ready to jump in with both feet, either way, rest assured that it will not take long before you experience a shift. You will likely begin to notice the difference immediately, but more importantly, after as little as one month, this will become such an ingrained part of your routine that continuing it will become easier than skipping it.

HAPPY MORNING CHECKLIST

- *Don't hit snooze*

If we want to create our day with intention and live it with joy and excitement, why would we want to wait one more second to wake up and live it? If you wake up by an alarm and the first act of the day is to hit snooze and go back to sleep, imagine that you are saying, "No thank you, universe. I'll choose to sleep through more of the magic I'm expecting today." If you knew it was going to be the best day of your life, you would jump out of bed to start experiencing it. So let's reverse engineer that by having that expectation create the habit and greeting the alarm clock as a welcomed friend who's reminding you that everything you want is waiting for you to wake up!

- *Tech delay*

Even though we know that our sleep will be better and more restful if we don't have our phones and devices in our rooms, many of us sleep with them right next to our beds. If you have not been able to part with the proximity of your tech, it would be helpful to have it in a drawer as opposed to right on the nightstand. But regardless of where that device is, one thing is certain. The moment you look at it, you will be confronted with an onslaught of information—of what the world is seeking from you or for you. You will see scrolls of headlines, get emails about work, social engagements, bills, and so forth. You will see texts and other notifications that will require or at least tempt your attention. The importance of this cannot be overstated. As we noted in the previous chapter, if you truly want to CREATE your day, you cannot do so in reaction mode. Instead, if you wait an hour before looking at your phone, the way you begin your day will improve immensely. This one act alone can have a huge impact. When not constantly distracted by a podcast or a news program or the ding of incoming messages, you will be more present to the people you live with, to the things you are doing, and you will feel less harried as you get on with the morning. It is almost impossible to feel present and distracted at once. You may be questioning if this is even possible; the messages you get and the information you are looking up may be important. What else is true is that whatever the world is seeking from you, they will still be seeking it in an hour. The difference is that the responses they will get will be from a more rooted, present, and energized you!

- ***Read your thirty-day letter***

In the previous chapter, you took the time to script the life of your dreams in thirty-day chunks in your thirty-day letter. We touched on the importance of reading it as the first act of the day. In this happy habit checklist, after waking up and resisting your tech for the first hour of your day, THIS is the perfect moment to fill your head and your heart with what you are seeking.

Read your letter.

- ***Drink water***

Research indicates that the average person loses between one-half to one liter of water during an eight-hour sleep cycle. Just like you see a plant come to life when it is watered, you will feel an immediate benefit from beginning your day with a big glass of water. If you prefer to drink it at room temperature, you may like to sleep with it next to your bed and enjoy your water as you read your letter. If you're a coffee junkie, fear not. This is not to suggest that you have water INSTEAD of coffee, but to have it BEFORE your morning cup o' joe. Not only does this help replenish the nightly dehydration but it is also an easy way to help you look rested and your skin look radiant.

- ***Move your body***

If you are wondering if your current workout routine counts, it does. Moving your body can mean different things to different people. The crucial point is that our bodies were designed to move. Perhaps you've heard the phrase "sitting is the new smoking." As humans have evolved and technology has emerged, we need to use less of our bodies to seek sustenance and shelter. Starting your day by moving can enhance your energy, improve your health, and serve as a reminder that you value this shell in which you live. Whether it's a walk around the block with your dog, a yoga class on YouTube, lifting weights in your bedroom, and so on—JUST MOVE! If you only have a few minutes, you still have time to do this. You could do jumping jacks or hold a plank. Those are examples of exercises that take very little time to change your physiology. But if you want to change your world, you MUST move your body.

- ***Connect with your soul***

The final step in our Happy Checklist is about connecting with YOU; the inner you, the YOUest you. This is an opportunity to feel grounded in that which brings you peace. If you pray, pray. If you meditate, meditate. (*If you'd like to meditate but don't know where to begin, go to www.joannarajendran.com and enter your email address. You will receive a complementary guided meditation.*) If you have no desire to do either of the above:

- Sit in silence
- Read an inspirational book (this one counts 😜)
- Think a kind thought about someone
- Write three things you're looking forward to
- Write three things you're grateful for
- Daydream

This is a beautiful chance to tune out so you can tune in—to disconnect with the stimulus of the outside world so that you can reconnect with who and how you are at your core. And from this place of peace, of presence, of power, you are primed and ready to go. . .

ROCK THE DAY!

CHAPTER 6
BEST.LIFE.EVER.

Inflating Your Bubble of Awesome

"You are the average of the five people you spend the most time with. Choose wisely."
—Jim Rohn

BEHAVIOR

Years ago, my then preteen niece was experiencing her first challenges when it came to her friend group. When trying to come up with a way to explain the importance of creating healthy boundaries in relationships, I told her to imagine a bubble around her. Inside that bubble lived everything that made her the most her: her humor, her kindness, her capacity for love, her unique magic. I said that in life, her biggest task will be to protect that bubble, and that while she can love everyone, not everyone in her world will deserve to be inside that special bubble.

In every connection there is an exchange of energy. In our lives, there will be people, events, and circumstances that increase that energy and others that will deplete it. Let's examine how we assess that and more importantly, what we do with that information to protect our most valuable resource: our energy.

 LESSON

INFLATORS

There are elements in our lives that metaphorically fill our bubbles. These are the friends who feel like sunshine, the adventures that fill our soul, the hobbies and passions we love, the professional pursuits we find richly rewarding. In terms of people, the INFLATORS feel like love in human form. After spending time with them, we leave feeling better, more alive, and happier than we did before. They are the people of whom we never tire, who we can pick up with after time apart without skipping a beat, who have the energy we desire to be around. When we hear from them, it feels delightful. The biggest indicator in determining those who inflate versus deflate our bubbles of awesome can be found in our feelings.

DEFLATORS

In contrast, a DEFLATOR is like an energy vampire. If we see their name scroll across our phone in the form of a call or message, we are not excited. In fact, you may even have the initial reaction to decline or ignore the call. We leave a DEFLATOR feeling less energized, less enthusiastic, and drained. Often we don't feel truly safe to be our most authentic self within these relationships.

And here's the kicker...

The categories are not fixed. It's possible that someone or something could be an inflator in one aspect of life and a deflator in another. Perhaps they are the first person to cheer you on professionally but judgmental when it comes to sharing the things of your heart. It could also shift with time. Some people will inflate your bubble in one season and deflate it in a different chapter of life. The key is identifying what's happening and having the tools to know what to do with that information.

Name five people in your life who fill your bubble. People with whom you love to talk, laugh, and share your most you, you. Your human sunshines.

_____
_____
_____
_____

Name five aspects of your professional life that are INFLATORS.

_____
_____
_____
_____

Last, name five hobbies or activities that fill you up.

_____
_____
_____
_____

Now, let's do the same thing with the DEFLATORS category. Name five people with whom you prefer not to engage; the people who feel like bubble poppers, who decrease the joy, happiness, and enthusiasm you experience while in their presence.

_____
_____
_____
_____

Name five aspects of your professional life that are DEFLATORS.

_____
_____
_____
_____

Name five tasks in your life that diminish your energy.

_____
_____
_____
_____
_____

🏋 EXERCISE

So now that we've covered the concept of protecting our bubbles of awesome and have identified some examples of people, events, and circumstances within our lives that fall into the categories of INFLATOR and DEFLATOR, what do we do with this information?

HEALTHY BOUNDARIES

The initial thought may be to eliminate the DEFLATORS in our lives. While a lofty goal, it may not always be practical or possible. Your DEFLATOR may be someone with whom you have to collaborate on a project at work, an ex-spouse with whom you coparent, or a task that is necessary to run your household (e.g., the endless cycle of laundry or cleaning toilets). Fear not. There will be times when cutting a DEFLATOR out of your life is not only possible, but it is also beneficial and necessary. There are others when limiting their access to you may help, and last, ways to train people how to treat you.

LIMITING ACCESS TO YOU

For the next seven days, choose a DEFLATOR in your life who you can remove. This doesn't have to be a permanent removal, but by eliminating their access for a week, you will begin to assess if the resulting impact is positive, negative, or neutral. For example, if it is a friend, consciously choose to not spend time or energy with this person for seven days; say no to plans, screen calls/texts, and so forth. If it is a household task that you can temporarily outsource, do so for the next week.

TAKING CONTROL OF THE ENERGY FLOW

For the DEFLATORS that cannot be removed for the next week, this is a great opportunity to practice conditioning those around you to treat you in the way you'd prefer. How do we do this? By controlling their access to us as though we are holding the velvet rope to the VIP area of our peace. For example, if you have an issue with a family member who constantly calls to complain or gossip about other people, you can still answer the phone. On the calls when they go to the negative behavior that you want less of, you have to end the call. In the conversations focused on the positive, you stay on the phone. You begin to energetically train the people in your world that they are granted more access to you when connecting with you in the way you prefer and less when they don't. (NOTE: *You are not trying to change the other person—you are setting the bar for healthy interactions in your specific relationship.*)

Chapter 7
BEST.LIFE.EVER.

Focus on Your Words

"Words are, in my not-so-humble opinion, our most inexhaustible source of magic."
—Albus Dumbledore (J. K. Rowling)

BEHAVIOR

"Hey, how are you?"
"Fine, thanks. How are you?"

What was wrong with that conversation?
Nothing, but what was right with it?
Also, nothing.

If we want to change the everyday interactions we have into moments of micro connections, we must consider the words that we use and especially those that we use most often. Left unchecked, a good portion of the conversations we have could be done by rote, on autopilot. Think of your own knee-jerk responses to the casual greeting above. Do you actually pause to consider how you feel and then answer accordingly, or do you have a polite response ready to roll?

If our words shape our world, it stands to reason that it makes sense to take an audit of those words we are thinking, especially those we say most often. As you examine your vocabulary, the landscape of your resulting world takes shape. You may notice an alarming yet empowering concept come into play: that the way you perceive your life and the words you use to describe it are directly related to the amount of pleasure you are deriving from living it.

If that is not clear enough, let's take this totally made-up example. Imagine a farmer who doesn't have much in the way of material goods or financial riches. Imagine that he loves being able to grow food, to watch the miracle of planting something, nurturing it, observing its transformation into actual sustenance, and being able to provide that for the betterment of the world. That farmer feels completely satisfied. In this example, the farmer is happy with his life, with his family, with his village or community, with his life. Imagine the words he may use to express such satisfaction. Now picture that same man, someone who loves to cultivate, to create, stuck in a cubicle, feeling like a cog in a bigger machine, where he doesn't feel like the cause he's contributing to makes a difference, and that his particular role within that contribution matters even less. Perhaps he has achieved a lot of financial reward for this path but isn't satisfied. He doesn't feel creative, excited, or like an enthusiastic participant in his own life. What words would you expect him to say about how he spends most of his time?

In the previous chapter, we examined the concept of INFLATORS versus DEFLATORS. Are the very words that most often come from your own mouth INFLATING or DEFLATING the experience of your own life?

📝 LESSON

THE WORDS YOU SAY

Pause. Close your eyes (well maybe read the rest of this and THEN close your eyes). Write down the words or phrases you say the most.

_____
_____
_____
_____
_____

Specifically, when asked throughout your day how you are, what is your current go-to response? (There are no wrong answers here, just starting points to identify if and how they are working for you.)

_____
_____
_____
_____
_____

Take a moment and reach out to five people very close to you and ask them to list the words they most associate with you. (These could be the words that pop into their minds as they think of you, but also be sure to ask them what words they notice you using the most. List them on the following page.)

_____
_____
_____
_____
_____

🏋 EXERCISE

THE REAL FOUR-LETTER WORDS

Taking into consideration the responses to the lesson above, now the fun can begin. For the next seven days, let's make an intention to maximize our everyday interactions into those real, impactful moments of connection. One of the simplest ways to do that is to let go of those four-letter words that are doing nothing to enhance our lives. What are those four-letter words? HINT: They are likely NOT the ones that first popped into your mind when you read that. The real four-letter words are:

OKAY   **FINE**   **GOOD**

Why? Because they have just taken what could be a point in your day where you exchange energy, kindness, and love and turned it into a robotic, canned moment of polite monotony.

If we take those four-letter words off the table, what is left for us to use throughout the day when we are asked how we are?

THE SEED WE WATER

When we stop answering automatically, we begin to respond authentically. That difference is EVERYTHING! It is when we feel true connection, real community, and present to our humanity. It is when we turn off the autopilot mode that we take back control of the moments of our lives.

- What's an example of something you could say when asked how you are if we aren't saying the four-letter responses mentioned above?
    - "I'm freaking amazing! Thank you so much for asking. How are YOU today?"
    - "This is the BEST DAY EVER, I just saw the most beautiful sunrise, and then while I was driving, the cutest turtle crossed the street in front of me."
    - "Peaceful and happy, thank you. Has your day been magical yet?"

Maybe reading those responses felt like a lot. If it's too sweet and sappy that you couldn't imagine saying anything like it, jot down some possible responses that could enroll people into your world in a positive way that sound like YOU.

_____
_____
_____
_____
_____
_____
_____

This is a question that comes up in every conversation about the power of words and specifically, within this exercise of how to respond to daily questions without the four-letter words. What if your day wasn't all rainbows and unicorns? Are you meant to lie in the spirit of (toxic) positivity?

NO.

If the intention is to have true moments of connection making for a more interconnected experience of your days, weeks, months and life, then we certainly don't need anything more than authenticity to accomplish that.

- Here are a few examples of how you could respond in one of those moments.
  - "My day has been total shit. But thank you for asking, this could be the moment it changes around. How are YOU today?"
  - "It has been freaking nuts, like hidden-camera-level crazy today. But who knows, maybe something magical is coming our way. How are YOU?"
  - "So far, this isn't my favorite day ever. But you are the first person who asked how I'm doing. So I'm thinking yours is the kindness that shifts the pattern. Thank you for changing my day. What's something awesome that has happened to you today?"

The goal isn't perfection; it isn't even positivity. The goal is CONNECTION.

Chapter 8
BEST.LIF**E**.EVER.

Expanding Your Practice

"We are what we repeatedly do. Excellence, then, is not an act, but a habit."
—*Aristotle*

Behavior

By this point in our journey together, you have hopefully used the tools in previous chapters to:

- Notice your behavior.
- Tune in and listen to your inner guides.
- Create your life with intention rather than react to what's presented.
- Establish healthy boundaries.
- Experience some meaningful shifts.

Let's pause for a moment and celebrate (fear not—we will have a full-blown party about your awesomeness at the end of the book). At this point, it's important to acknowledge you; the decision to begin this journey, the commitment to stick with it, and the results you've already created. Celebration inspires continuation, which is why we shall return to the party vibes at the completion of our time together.

For now, however, let's take the opportunity to go a bit deeper into your new arsenal of happiness habits or what I like to call, *happy hacks*.

📝 LESSON

Let's begin by getting to know this version of you a bit more intimately; what brings you joy, what gives you peace, what sets your soul on fire.

I feel most myself when I'm...

_____
_____
_____
_____
_____

The five people in my life who make me laugh the most are...

_____
_____
_____
_____
_____

Something I truly love about myself that I'd like to express more of is...

_____
_____
_____
_____
_____

My favorite form of meditation is...

_____
_____
_____
_____
_____

♟ EXERCISE
BREATHWORK

The benefits to having a breathwork practice are numerous and include the following: reducing stress, depression, chronic pain; improving lung health, increasing energy and attention span; boosting digestive and immune systems; and healing from trauma. If many of us are aware of the stated benefits, why isn't this something that we schedule, consistently and intentionally, daily? For many of us, it comes down to not knowing where to start or to thinking we don't have enough time. We tend to put our time, money, and energy into what we value. Hopefully, by this point in our time together, you are valuing YOU; knowing with your whole heart that putting the effort into you being your YOUest YOU will add love and value to your family, your community, your world. So where do we begin if we'd like to experience the benefits of breathwork?

Inhale a big, long breath and PAUSE. Feel the sensation of being completely full, and then exhale with a noisy, full-body sigh. Allow your face to let go of tension, your shoulders to soften, your body to relax.

Well done! If you notice, it doesn't take much to change our physiological state. As my mentor and the world's oldest yoga teacher, Tao, used to say when she taught, "Taking one good breath in yoga will add a year to your life without pain." Is it true? I don't know, but she did live (and dance) until the ripe old age of 101! So let's choose to believe as we experiment with the following three different types of breathwork.

- ***BOX BREATHING***

    o   WHY—To help you relax, calm the mind, and lower your levels of cortisol (the stress hormone).

    o   HOW—Also known in yoga as *sama vritti pranayama*, or even the 4x4 breathing technique, box breathing uses imagery of a square. It is simple and effective. You inhale for a count of four, pause

for a count of four, exhale for a count of four, pause for a count of four.
  - TIP—Counting is a helpful technique in meditation as it is hard to count and focus on other things at the same time. Should you find it difficult to count or remember where you are in the box breath, you can use a "tapping" of the thumb to the other fingers of the same hand, that is inhale one (thumb touches index finger), two (thumb touches middle finger), three (thumb touches ring finger), and four (thumb touches pinky).

- **BREATH OF FIRE**
  - WHY—To boost brain function, enhance digestion, strengthen your core, and improve respiratory health.
  - HOW—Also referred to in Sanskrit as *Kapalabhati*, the breath of fire is used in Kundalini Yoga to cleanse and energize the mind, body, and soul. Fire breathing uses a passive inhale and a forceful exhale that pushes onto the diaphragm, releasing the air from the lungs quickly out through your nostrils.
  - TIP—This is a more advanced breath practice that may have contraindications for some groups of people. Though I love this style of breathwork generally, do a bit of research to ensure that this would be a safe addition for you personally. Also, be sure to blow your nose prior to beginning.

- **UJJAYI BREATH**
  - WHY—To build inner heat, boost vitality, increase focus and concentration, and encourage cleansing.
  - HOW—If you've ever taken a yoga class and heard the Darth Vader-like breathing of those around you, you are already familiar with the Ujjayi breath. A pranayama technique that makes

your breathing sound like an ocean, *Ujjayi* (a Sanskrit term typically translated to mean "victorious breath") can be practiced by constricting the back of your throat while inhaling and exhaling through your nose.

- o   TIP—If you have trouble constricting the glottis (or even knowing what or where that is), this should help. Hold your hand in front of your face and make a *haaa* breath as though you are going to fog a mirror. Make the *haaa* sound on both the inhale and the exhale. Once you find it, close your mouth and continue making that sound, engaging the back of the throat, even while breathing through the nose.

GUIDED MEDITATION

In addition to the breathwork, if you would like to expand your meditation practice but prefer to be guided, visit www.joannarajendran.com and sign up for our mailing list. You will immediately receive a **FREE** guided meditation.

TAO'S MEDITATION

As an added bonus, I will share, in written form, Tao Porchon-Lynch's guided meditation that she used in savasana to complete every class and workshop she taught. You can find one of her CDs to hear it in her voice, or you may wish to record it and be guided by your own:

Lie down on the ground in a perfectly balanced position, your feet slightly apart, arms outstretched, the palms facing upward. Feel the space between the shoulders and buttocks, shut your eyes, and try and let go of the outer world, your thoughts, and the mental pictures that invade the mind.

Tune into the lingering sun as with an explosion of colors, it brilliantly lights up the sky, then gently bids farewell as it sinks beyond the horizon.

Surrender your whole being to the silence that seems to creep over the earth as dusk falls, and listen suddenly to the rhythm of stillness. You can experience the vibrations of energy as you surrender deeper and deeper into the ground.

Witness the belly and the pelvis rise and fall with your breath . . . become the breath. The fire of creation of the solar plexus seems to glow like the setting sun. Your breath becomes deep, yet simple, like a cloud hanging in space. The mind, now soft, seems to merge within that space. Listen to the pulse beat of the earth, become one with your heart.

Be the earth.

Glide on the sound of your breath, like a seagull glides and seems to float over the ocean. Your breath seems to have wings as you become one with your inner self.

Allow the skin of your face and forehead to relax. Relax the corners of your mouth. Swallow. Soften the tongue as gently your breath is drawn through the subtle tissues of the body. Sense the broadness of your being as your entire body appears to melt into space. The waves of your breath seem to float into oneness with the eternal energy. And know that you are that energy.

Allow the muscles of the shoulders, neck, and spinal column to melt into the stillness of universal peace, completely surrendering the physical body, letting go of your conscious mind. You seem to drift through space, through the door of life into the universal timeless power of the eternal. For you have opened the door of this internal power and feel the miracle within yourself as you witness the renewal of the body and mind, and relax.

Yogis believe that a new cycle begins every day as we become aware of this rejuvenation process.

Each rung of the ladder of life relates to the various chakras within the body. As you let go through this passage of timelessness, like the cycle of the sun and the moon, you are like the endless tides of the ocean, constantly flowing in and out, cleansing every cell in your body, every organ renewing. You become conscious that you have reached another dimension, one with this cosmic ocean wherein the power of the universe is deep and the silence never disturbed and the mind is brought to rest in the cradle of your heart.

CHAPTER 9
BEST.LIFE.EVER.

Empowering Partnerships

"Individually, we are one drop. Together, we are an ocean."
—Ryunosuke Satoro

BEHAVIOR

Have you ever made a New Year's resolution only to discover you might not have been as "resolved" as initially predicted before the clock struck midnight? Perhaps you had every intention to read more books, go to that fitness class, ditch social media for a month, try a dry January, and so on. Whether it happened on January first or at any other time during the year, chances are that you can relate to the notion of setting a goal, creating a new habit, or forming a new intention only to have your mind, your time, your people, your LIFE get in the way. How do I know? Because if you're human, you have likely experienced doing this both successfully and unsuccessfully so far in your life.

So what makes the difference? Why is it the case that sometimes, we can make a massive shift one simple choice at a time and others, we find we fall off before we begin? There can be a lot of factors that influence the outcome, yet there is one pervasive theme that seems to underscore the successes.

What is it? you wonder.

Glad you asked. Not only is it something that costs nothing and is readily available, but it's also something you likely have access to already. It's a . . . (insert drumroll in your mind please) . . . PARTNER!

✎ LESSON

If you've ever experienced any of the examples of new habits successfully broken or created, chances are high that you didn't succeed alone. Let's use the fitness example. Why does it make such a difference to enhance your personal health to have a partner? If you've ever had a "workout buddy," you will likely agree that the benefit of partnership was huge. Such benefits include:

- INCREASED JOY
- BUILT-IN ACCOUNTABILITY
- MORE ENCOURAGEMENT
- SAFE SPACE TO COURSE CORRECT
- SHARED CELEBRATION

Having a partner gives you a safe space to imagine a future that is different from your current reality. It gives you an outlet to speak your dreams and goals into existence... and there's added power in saying them aloud. This partnership will help you focus on the desired goal, shortening the amount of time it takes you to get there. And best yet, your growth, and the speed of that growth, will be faster by having these conversations regularly.

HOW TO CHOOSE A PARTNER

DO

- ***CHOOSE A PARTNER WHO:***
    - **Has similar values**—Note that it says values and not goals. While your goal might be professional and your partner may be working on a personal one, as long as what you value is similar, it could be a beneficial partnership.
    - **Will be transparent and vulnerable with you**—A partnership will only be beneficial to the degree that it is authentic. It is imperative that you and your partner believe that the other has

your best interest at heart and wants to see you win. While you don't want a partner who will blow smoke unjustifiably, you do want one who will be your biggest cheerleader.

- **Will remind you who you are when you forget**—Whenever we attempt to go for something, there will be times when the going gets tough and the desire to quit will be strong. You may forget why you even started. This will be when you see how crucial it is that you have chosen a partner with the courage and confidence to call bullshit and to help you get back on your path.

DO NOT ✗

- ***CHOOSE A PARTNER WHO:***

    - **Is already super close to you**—It's not always easy to embark on something. When creating a new habit or going for a goal, we are putting ourselves out in the world in a vulnerable way. Our relationships are already layered with the shared experiences we've had throughout our time together. When you seek a partner who has a bit of distance from you, this goal, or both, you are able to be supported by someone who has the perspective of distance.

    - **Will judge you**—Your dreams, your goals, and your life is sacred and should be treated as such. Saying any of them out loud, let alone going for them, takes courage. You need to know that you can say anything to your partner without reservation. You'll want an environment of creation, of support, and most importantly, free of preconceived notions or judgments.

    - **Is just like you**—There is so much value in having a partner with different or complementary strengths than those that you possess. For example, if you are a big thinker, it may be valuable to partner with someone who may dream big but work small. Their detail-oriented nature could help you view the path through a different lens.

🏋 EXERCISE
LET'S FIND YOU A PARTNER

The challenge for this chapter is to identify something in your life you would like to commit to for the next seven days and then choose a partner to enhance the experience. In terms of the commitment, it could be a professional goal, a health-related one, a commitment to going tech-free for an hour a day, adding a morning ritual, a practice of gratitude, and so on. It matters less what the specific intention is than it does that we are practicing using the power of partnerships.

Why is the partner so important? To recap, when chosen well, our partners can:

- Remind us why we started when we feel like giving up
- Check in with us if we forget to connect with them
- Cheer us on amplifying the joy of the wins
- Do it with us

A practice/habit/goal that I'm committing to for the next seven days is . . .

_____
_____
_____
_____
_____
_____
_____

Now that you've chosen your intention, let's consider someone in your world who would be a good fit for this challenge.

Who do you know that would do this with you, committing to a goal for the next seven days? (*Remember, the goals could differ—the support is the aspect you'll share.*)

Chapter 9: Empowering Partnerships

_____
_____
_____
_____
_____
_____

Fantastic! You have selected both the commitment and the partner candidate. So what's next?

ASK AND YOU SHALL RECEIVE

Once you've narrowed your candidates down to a short list above, take a look and begin with the person you deem to be the best fit—your first choice. Then, ask them. Sometimes people get a little weird here. I've found the best approach to be the simplest. Reach out and let them know that you are committing to something in your life for the next seven days, and you would love to partner with them if they are open. You can ask if there's anything in their world that they would like to commit to during the same time period and if it would work to connect via daily check-ins. An ancillary benefit of this is that it often inspires the other person to choose something that they may have been thinking about or meaning to do and now have the support to jump in.

AS NIKE SAID . . . JUST DO IT

Once your partner agrees, it helps to identify the preferred method of check-in. For example, if you're both phone people, maybe you choose a time each day to connect via traditional phone call or over video call. If your goal is somewhat straightforward, such as going for a daily jog, you may choose to text once complete. Clients in the past used accountability partners as an outlet for their three morning gratitudes and would begin each day by texting new ones. One of my favorite accountability partnerships was done almost exclusively by voice memos. That's a great feature because the partner hears your words in your voice and with your tone, sharing thoughts, insights, and updates. But unlike a phone call, the other partner doesn't have to be available to hear it. They can simply listen when they get to the message and reply as convenient.

The best part is that once you connect with the massive impact that such partnerships can and will have in terms of your goal, and more importantly, in terms of your life, you will be inspired to take advantage of this in other aspects of your world.

CHAPTER 10
BEST.LIFE.EVER.

Virtue of Giving It Away (Pay It Forward)

"We make a living by what we get. We make a life by what we give."
—Winston Churchill

BEHAVIOR

Whether it was a birthday surprise, a Christmas gift we'd been hoping for, or something we worked hard to buy ourselves, most of us can relate to the feeling of wanting something and then the satisfaction of receiving it. The process of what initially was a THOUGHT in our minds turned into a THING in our lives. It can feel like an answered prayer, a realized dream. And when we're young, it can certainly feel like the ultimate of satisfying experiences.

Then, at some point, we get to experience how amplified the feeling of satisfaction becomes when we are able to GIVE that feeling to someone else. We learn that giving that gift that someone has always dreamed of can be even more rewarding than receiving our own. We learn that directing our love, our thoughtfulness, our kindness outward is even more delicious.

So far, in our time together, we have used thoughts, rituals, and practices to create new habits in our lives. These exercises can cause life-changing shifts, and that is very exciting. So now, let's practice using these new tools and shifting the focus outward.

Why?

Because if what you've already done feels good, wait until you feel how incredible it feels to harness and then focus that same magic on others.

And even better?

We will do so anonymously to connect with the joy of giving for the sake of the giving.

✏️ LESSON

So how do you choose the subject of this practice of generosity?

Who is someone in your world who leaves people feeling better than they found them? Someone who is the first to think of others? Perhaps it is someone in your immediate world, someone who shows up for you—the kind of friend or family member who would drop everything to help you move that piece of furniture, give you a ride when your car breaks down, come running when you need a kind hug or a listening ear. Who is the person (or people) who popped into mind when reading that?

_____
_____
_____
_____
_____

Maybe the person you focus your energy on this week isn't someone you know well. Perhaps it's a colleague, the kind person who works the checkout at your neighborhood supermarket or the local mail carrier. Is there someone in your daily life who goes the extra mile to do things with love to put a smile on the faces of those around them? List them as possible candidates here.

_____
_____
_____
_____
_____

The great news is that in this act of kindness, it matters less who you choose than it does that you give yourself the gift of this experience. It is through this generosity of spirit that we connect with our true, most altruistic nature.

So, take a glance at the names you've compiled and choose one. No worries if narrowing it down proved challenging as once you begin this practice, it is one you will likely want to continue.

EXERCISE
HOW TO START

In previous chapters, we have practiced habits of manifesting, of creating, of focusing on what we most want to be, give, have, or do. So what is the big shift in directing that same energy outward to someone else? In doing so, we are taking these skills and getting better at them. When we are using our imagination to focus on someone else's dreams being realized, we are likely to be more playful in our asks and more patient in the unfolding as we are less personally attached to the result.

If you know the person well enough to know what they desire, you can spend the next seven days praying, visualizing, or meditating on the most satisfying version of what they seek. For example, if someone in your family is going through a health issue, you may see them thriving in total health with beautiful, vibrant cells. If you have a dear friend who expressed loneliness, you may see them totally in love. You could even imagine them calling you to tell you all about their excitement. If you don't know the person well, as in the example of a coworker or someone you know casually in your community, your kindness can be just as meaningful even if less specific. You could see them getting back the love and energy they give out tenfold. You could radiate your appreciation to and for them as you think about them.

CREATE A RITUAL

Creating a ritual or a habit around this challenge can help ensure that you do it regularly, intentionally, and whole-heartedly for the entirety of the challenge. That doesn't mean that it has to be time-consuming. You can choose a part of your day to dedicate to them. Whether you spend five minutes after waking imagining the best for your person or if you decide to use your commute as their special time, the important thing is that you have a dedicated method and time of day.

SURPRISE & DELIGHT

This part of the challenge has tended to be a "fan favorite" from those who have participated in **BEST.LIFE.EVER. the course**. They love taking the time to come up with and then put into action their method of surprise and delight. As the name implies, as part of our acts of kindness and love, we include a surprise gesture, thought, or gift. It could range in cost, scale, or delivery, but the common denominator is the thoughtfulness from the giver and the delight from the receiver. Previous examples include:

- A kindergarten teacher decided to choose the woman who worked in the cafeteria at her school. The day before we had our session, the teacher realized that all the kids in school called this woman "the lunch lady." When she asked for her name so that the kids could address her more personally, she was touched and shared her name but was also quick to say that it was OK that they called her "lunch lady." The teacher spent the next seven days thinking of her and seeing her receive the kindness she doled out with each serving of food to every student. She saw her happy. She saw her thriving. And as a special surprise and delight, she ordered a personalized nametag to give to the woman.

- A woman in my own family is a matriarch—a mother and grandmother to many kids and a sparkly souled human. She is always exuding love and kindness to those around her. When she moved into an independent living place, she brought that generous spirit with her, befriending everyone, advocating for those who needed it and even creating a library for the residents. I initially thought to donate books to her library when an inside source told me that for some of the residents, the font in the books was too small for them to read. It gave me the perfect idea to send whole-page magnifiers that could be used interchangeably with all the books in their collection.

- While Amazon and online shopping does make it more accessible to gift anonymously, the gift doesn't need to be financial or material to be thoughtful. Some of the best examples have been handwritten notes of gratitude or letters of appreciation—heartfelt and unsigned.

SHHH...

By now, I'm sure you appreciate the value of this activity, but you may be wondering what the big deal is with all the secrecy. Maybe you get it theoretically, but just wait until you experience it practically. Sending the kindness from your heart to another, using the power of your mind for another, and using the resources of your generosity for another, is a powerful thing. It connects with the power of your love. It reminds us that the only thing better than giving is giving for the sake of giving! By removing the opportunity for acknowledgment, we connect with the magnitude of doing the deed for the deed's sake.

RECRUIT & REPEAT

This is a powerful activity and one you're sure to enjoy over the next seven days. But it doesn't have to end there. Years ago, when my daughter was very young, we started a ritual that every Wednesday we would have surprise and delight moments. They included:

- Leaving a $20 bill in the nozzle of the pump at a gas station.
- Hiding some money and an encouraging note in a self-help book in a bookstore.
- Paying for the car behind me on the Starbucks drive-through line.

These were meaningful moments, and my daughter got to witness, at a very young age, how powerful and far-reaching the ripple of kindness could be. In the bookstore example, she asked what would happen if the note and money were found by someone who worked at the shop rather than a shopper. I assured her that whoever was meant to find it was the one meant to be blessed by it. With the Starbucks example, she wanted to witness the joy even if it was meant to be anonymous, so I told her we could pull over into the corner of the parking lot and wait for the next person to pull up. But the real moment had already happened as my daughter saw that the joy we meant to spread to the next customer had already spread to the two baristas working there. Shocked that I had no personal order, they couldn't believe that we pulled in simply to make someone else's day. So while the "gift" wasn't for the baristas, we did leave them with a big tip and a great reminder of how their own kindness could spread.

If this feels so good in the next seven days that you don't want to stop, DON'T! Either continue with the same person or choose a new one and keep going. If those in your world know what you're up to, encourage them to choose their own person and do it with you. While the goal is to keep the recipient from knowing you are their benefactor, doing this with others is a great way to compound the kindness.

CHAPTER 11
BEST.LIFE.EVER.

Emerging As I Am

"An affirmation opens the door. It's a beginning point on the path to change."
—Louise Hay

BEHAVIOR

The most powerful declaration we make are the words that follow "I AM." Left unchecked, we can end that sentence without being conscious of how what we're saying shapes who we are and how we move through this world. The words you use can lift you up, can highlight your unique gifts, or they can dim your own light making your power smaller. The world responds to the version of ourselves that we present.

If you are an adult, you may remember your first real job. When we embark on a new career, when is it that we truly embody that new role? Is it when we see our name on a business card? Is it when we start wearing the clothes we associate with that job? Or is it when we start introducing ourselves and include that title?

How often do the roles that we play become intertwined with our notions of who we are in this world: a parent, a friend, a sibling, a writer, a teacher, an artist, and so on? In that way, who we are is more who we think we are in relation to those other people in our lives.

So, if we've uncovered what it is that we want to BE, GIVE, DO, or HAVE more of in life, what does that mean in terms of who we are? Also, once we let go of the notions of self that no longer serve us, what is left? Let's play with the following questions to get more clarity around this.

📝 LESSON

BEFORE

I've always been told I'm too . . .

_____
_____
_____
_____
_____
_____

Everyone says I'm so good at . . .

_____
_____
_____
_____
_____
_____

The way I hid from feeling less than was . . .

_____
_____
_____
_____
_____
_____

PAUSE

Let's take a moment to close your eyes, to breathe, to center. Take a big breath in and slowly sigh out the exhale. The questions you just answered were the things you've likely been carrying around for a while. The intention behind this book is to stop the autopilot of habitual thought and action and to begin consciously curating the thoughts, feelings, and experiences we want to have going forward. So let this pause serve you before continuing. If the breath worked, great. Keep going. If you need more, do some jumping jacks, take a dance break, walk your dog, sit in nature, and so on. Make sure that it is from that energetic, clean slate that you answer the next few questions and then jump into the exercise.

NOW

Who I really am in my soul is . . .

_____
_____
_____
_____
_____
_____

I commit to showing up in the world as . . .

_____
_____
_____
_____
_____
_____

What I love about myself is . . .

_____
_____
_____
_____
_____
_____

🏋 Exercise

Affirmations are one of the tools that we can use to build and strengthen this muscle of identity; to decide who we are and then live into that notion. Based on the responses to the previous questions, let's jot down a few possible affirmations.

_____
_____
_____
_____
_____
_____

If you find it helpful, here are some ideas of simple affirmations you may wish to use in addition to your own:

- I am love
- I am loved
- I am healthy, wealthy, and wise
- Everything I seek is seeking me
- I am whole
- I am kind
- I am beautiful
- Money flows to me with ease
- I am blessed
- I am inspired
- I inspire
- I am worthy

STRIKE A POSE

Notice your posture right this moment. How are you standing or sitting? Are your shoulders hunched or are they tall and proud? Are your arms open and relaxed or crossed protectively or defensively? Are your legs crossed or are both feet grounded and connected to the earth? Posture is a shortcut to power. There are both physiological and psychological benefits to standing tall and proud.

When using affirmations, it's beneficial to stand in front of a mirror so that you can watch and hear yourself saying these words to and for you. As you stand, make sure that your feet are hip distance apart. Keep your arms and hands relaxed by your side. Bring your shoulders up, back, and down so that you release tension from your head, neck, shoulders, and back. Feel open in your heart and across your chest.

SAY IT

Using affirmations as a daily practice is an effective way of reminding yourself who you are and what you value. We are using our words to train our brains on what to think about, specifically as it pertains to our notions of self and identity. Too often, the words that repeat in our heads are in a critical voice. We are going to use affirmations to train that voice to be our raving fan. Will it happen immediately? Unlikely. But if we continue this ritual until it becomes a habit, the chances are high that we will begin to believe and live into our own words.

REPEAT IT

To begin, you can either choose one phrase and repeat it like a mantra. A mantra is a word or phrase said repeatedly to help cultivate mindfulness, concentration, and self-awareness. Or you can choose a handful of different affirmations and go through them one at a time. Remember, for maximum benefits, you will want to say these OUT LOUD to your own image while standing in your power pose. Ideally, we want to say our affirmations pretty soon after waking.

Then it becomes a touchstone that we can turn to as we go about the rest of the day. For added magic, some clients have chosen to record themselves saying their affirmations so that they have them to play back as needed.

CHAPTER 12
BEST.LIFE.EVER.

Relive & Recap

"Memory . . . is the diary that we all carry about with us."
—Oscar Wilde

BEHAVIOR

Hopefully, throughout the course of this book, you have released some of what no longer serves and have utilized the lessons and exercises within these pages to amplify and create what you seek. When we want more of something, it pays to recognize it. In that way, *celebration* can lead to *continuation*. We will use this final chapter as a way to relive and recap the general topics and your specific takeaways from the work you've already done.

LESSON

It has been noted that when you compete in a marathon, you are most likely to quit when you hit your "marathon wall," which could range anywhere around mile eighteen to mile twenty-three. Why? What is it about that stretch? In the beginning of anything, we can use excitement and enthusiasm to fuel us. When we see the finish line, we can use will and determination to realize the goal. But somewhere along the way, you will relate to what many experience at their marathon wall—feeling like you've been running forever but have still not arrived.

Can you relate to this marathon example? Are there things in your life that you've been committed to long enough that frustration has ensued over it not happening yet? And if so, if we know and expect this quit-or-commit moment to arise, what can we do to overcome it? Spoiler alert—everything you've already practiced throughout this book, and what we do in **BEST. LIFE.EVER. the course** is for this exact benefit. Let's use the exercise portion here to remind you how far you've come and to cheer you across the finish line. Will this be the last time? As long as you're alive and creating, manifesting, building—these tools will be yours to rinse and repeat.

🏋 EXERCISE

CH1 - BE PRESENT
TOWARD/AWAY

Your takeaway from this chapter . . .

_____
_____
_____
_____
_____
_____

A habit of thought/behavior you'd like to continue . . .

_____
_____
_____
_____
_____
_____
_____

CH2 - EXORCISE LIMITING BELIEFS
TRAUMA LETTER EXERCISE

Your takeaway from this chapter . . .

_____
_____
_____
_____
_____
_____

A habit of thought/behavior you'd like to continue . . .

_____
_____
_____
_____
_____
_____

CH3 - (4) STEPS TO MANIFESTING ASK. BELIEVE. RELEASE. THANK.

Your takeaway from this chapter . . .

_____
_____
_____
_____
_____
_____
_____

A habit of thought/behavior you'd like to continue . . .

_____
_____
_____
_____
_____
_____

Chapter 12: Relive & Recap

CH4 - THIRTY-DAY LETTER
THIRTY-DAY LETTER EXERCISE

Your takeaway from this chapter . . .

___

A habit of thought/behavior you'd like to continue . . .

___

CH5 - LET'S CREATE THE DAY
THE MORNING RITUAL

Your takeaway from this chapter . . .

___

A habit of thought/behavior you'd like to continue...

CH6 - INFLATING THE BUBBLE OF AWESOME
INFLATORS/DEFLATORS

Your takeaway from this chapter . . .

A habit of thought/behavior you'd like to continue . . .

CH7 - FOCUS ON YOUR WORDS
HARNESSING THE POWER OF LANGUAGE

Your takeaway from this chapter . . .

_____
_____
_____
_____
_____
_____
_____

A habit of thought/behavior you'd like to continue . . .

_____
_____
_____
_____
_____
_____
_____

CH8 - EXPANDING YOUR PRACTICE
ACCESSING YOUR PEACE

Your takeaway from this chapter . . .

_____
_____
_____
_____
_____
_____
_____

A habit of thought/behavior you'd like to continue . . .

CH9 - EMPOWERING PARTNERSHIPS
THE POWER OF ACCOUNTABILITY

Your takeaway from this chapter . . .

A habit of thought/behavior you'd like to continue . . .

CH10 - **V**IRTUE OF GIVING IT AWAY
DIRECTING THE MAGIC OUTWARD

Your takeaway from this chapter . . .

_____
_____
_____
_____
_____
_____
_____

A habit of thought/behavior you'd like to continue . . .

_____
_____
_____
_____
_____
_____
_____

CH11 - **E**MERGING AS I AM
THE POWER OF AFFIRMATIONS

Your takeaway from this chapter . . .

_____
_____
_____
_____
_____
_____
_____

A habit of thought/behavior you'd like to continue . . .

_____
_____
_____
_____
_____
_____
_____

CH12 - RELIVE & RECAP
THE POWER OF CELEBRATION

Overall, this experience has shifted me . . .

_____
_____
_____
_____
_____
_____
_____

I'm most proud of myself for . . .

_____
_____
_____
_____
_____
_____

Epilogue
Dream On

So now you know. You know the things that light your soul on fire. You are clear on the version of your life that is your **BEST.LIFE.EVER.** The remaining question is, what are you going to do about it?

When we practice experiencing our lives more presently and more positively, it impacts our relationship with ourselves, our families, our friends, our coworkers, our communities. How we go out into the world is different. Our interactions are more meaningful, our connections more connected.

The ripple this will have will spread wider than you will likely ever know or could possibly imagine. The shine of your light will be a beacon for others to turn theirs on, brightly and unapologetically.

REPEAT AS NEEDED

The best teachers are always learning, the best athletes are always training, and the best coaches are always being coached.

After the first ever session of **BEST.LIFE.EVER.** years ago, I was surprised that more than half of the group wanted to sign up for the next round. Even after I made sure they knew it would be the same content that they just experienced. And yet, they wanted in. When asked why, the answers were one of the following two responses:

- o "I didn't really know this would work so I played a little small. I want to do it again and go bigger!"

- "I loved the feeling I had doing it and especially doing it with a group of like-minded people. I would just miss my weekly check-in."

Those inaugural participants tapped into something immediately—creating a life with passion and purpose attracts us to others who are doing the same. The result is an elevation in the conversations you have, the friends you make, the fun you experience. Your YOUness is on bold display.

Sometimes we go back and reread a book we loved, and this time around we get something new out of it. The book didn't change. Who we are and where we are is the variable that changed. Now, years later, there have been alumni of **BEST.LIFE.EVER.** who have retaken the course multiple times per year. As we grow, what we are seeking is shifting. Sometimes people come back to this content to manifest something new, to gather with a mastermind of people who support one another, or to reengage with habits of happiness and success.

This book is yours to revisit—as needed—to remind yourself who you are in those moments when you forget.

THE MISSING PEACE

It is my absolute honor to be a small part of your path to peace, to joy, to satisfaction. Remember that as you continue on your journey, there are many ways we can stay connected.

- On my website www.joannarajendran.com, you may enter your email address to receive a free guided meditation and to join our virtual community.
- You can participate in the next round of the inspiration behind this book: **BEST.LIFE.EVER. the course.**
- Check out **The Manifest Station** podcast that I cohost with my partner Jen Rubinetti on Spotify or Apple Music.
- Grab a copy of my first book *My Guru Wears Heels* on amazon.com.
- Join us on our next immersive **BEtreat or WEtreat** experience.
- Feel free to email me your wins and magical moments or to book me to connect with your community at **therajendrangroup@outlook.com**.

Acknowledgments

"I'd like to thank the academy on this auspicious occasion..."

That was the beginning of the Oscar acceptance speech that my Aunt Judy taught my sister Jen, my brother Jonny, and me from the time we learned to speak. Had any of us even expressed a slight interest in the profession of acting? NOPE. Was "auspicious" an easy word for young children to pronounce? Also, NOPE. But such was Aunt Ju's belief in each of us that she wanted us to be prepared and gracious when the time came that we would be appreciated for using our respective gifts. When publishing my first book, she said she wanted to pay for the cover design so that she could be "part of my success." You may not be here physically this time around, but JuJu, you will always be a part of it all. I know that when I miss you, I will still hear your famously cranky voice in my mind bossing me around.

Being raised in such an environment, surrounded and supported by love, guidance, and joy, impacted every aspect of my life.

Thank you to my OGs, my mom Ilene (who we call Bo) and my dad Alan (my Atticus). My mom instilled, in each of us, a true curiosity and love of fellow humans. My dad has taught us the importance of integrity and expressing ourselves through writing (as long as we did so with proper grammar!). To have parents who celebrate your weirdness and believe in your path is the greatest gift. You have managed to be the unicorns: divorced best friends who, along with the best stepmother Shirlee, are there for and with each other and the family through every phase of life. At each milestone, family dinner, and holiday, you have modeled what is possible when the focus is love.

Thanks to my siblings and step siblings, our family (and my heart) keep expanding. To my many nieces and nephews: Jada, Sean, Jessica, Jax, Daniel, Macy, Charlie, Colton, Hadley, Julian, and Ryder . . . Aunt JoJo loves you bigger than the universe!

To my siblings, the other two of the three Js . . . there's no Jo without a Jen and a Jonny. You have been and will be forever my greatest friends, my best hugs, and my biggest laughs. Thank God we all married people who not only get this, but who have also chosen to jump into the madness on purpose. Thank you Chris and Bethy . . . period.

Years ago, I wrote a list to the universe with about eighty-one qualities that I wanted in my forever person. My Dude, thank you for being 79.5 of them. (Speaks another language is the half because he can still learn . . . but punctual must have been misspelled!) You have the amazing ability to ground me without ever clipping my wings, to believe in my ideas even when you don't get them, and to love me—unconditionally and completely. You are awkwardly honest, plan the best dates, and have secretly saved every card or note I've ever given you. You are my BIG LOVE, and I love being Your Girl.

To my fiery powerhouse Natasha Tao, you have the strength, intelligence, and emotional fortitude to change the world. You have more courage and confidence than anyone I know, and on days when I forget my own power, you remind me. I love watching you shine as you navigate this life.

River Vail, our animal-obsessed, constantly dancing, people-loving boy. You completed our family and added to the magic of the whole world by being born. Your kind heart, empathy, and capacity to love is so beyond your years. You blow our minds with your brilliance—seeing the world through the lens of a curious artist. May you keep blessing us and everyone you meet with your silliness and smile for the rest of your days.

Thank you, Gayle, for continuing Bill's legacy and for getting what it is that I was put here to do. You, Josh, Kenneth, and your incredible Waterside team have helped me turn my dream into my reality.

www.ingramcontent.com/pod-product-compliance
Lightning Source LLC
LaVergne TN
LVHW051847080426
835512LV00018B/3115